Come Closer

Sarah Fleming

Sam Si...
1360 Mona...
Denver, Colorado
United States
Planet Earth
Solar System
Universe

Contents

The Universe   2
The Solar System   4
Earth   6
The United States   8
Denver   10
Sam's House   12
Sam   14
Look Back   15
Index   15
Glossary   16

Trackers

Do you do this in your books?
Let's look at my address.

Sam Singh
1360 Monaco Street
Denver, Colorado
United States
Planet Earth
Solar System
Universe

The Hubble Space Telescope took this photo. It shows only a small part of the **universe**.

HUBBLE SPACE TELESCOPE

 Let's start big...
The universe is very, very, VERY big.
It is billions of **light years** across.

Sam Singh
1360 Monaco Street
Denver, Colorado
United States
Planet Earth
Solar System
Universe

We live in the **solar system**. Earth is the third **planet** from the Sun.

Sun   **Venus**   **Mars**

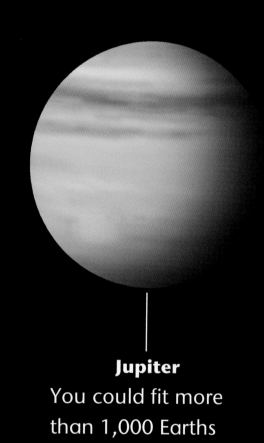

Mercury   **Earth**

The Earth is small, isn't it?

Jupiter

You could fit more than 1,000 Earths into Jupiter. It is BIG!

This is not a photo. An artist drew this diagram on a computer.

Saturn

Neptune

Uranus

Pluto

This diagram shows the planets closer together than they really are. The solar system is about 6,000,000,000 miles (10,000,000,000 km) wide.

Come Closer

Sam Singh
1360 Monaco Street
Denver, Colorado
United States
Planet Earth
Solar System
Universe

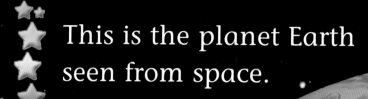

This is the planet Earth seen from space.

This is the shape of the United States. Find it in the photo.

Look for the clouds.

This photo was taken from a spacecraft.

Earth is about 8,000 miles (12,800 km) wide.

Come Closer

Sam Singh
1360 Monaco Street
Denver, Colorado
United States
Planet Earth
Solar System
Universe

 I live in the United States.

Look for the big lakes
and mountains.

I live in a city
called Denver.

This part is Colorado.

Colorado

The United States is big!
It covers more than
3,537,441 square miles
(9,161,930 km squared).

This picture was taken from a **satellite**.

North

West — East

South

Come Closer

Sam Singh
1360 Monaco Street
Denver, Colorado
United States
Planet Earth
Solar System
Universe

Look at the photo and the map.
Can you see some of the city
of Denver?

Photo

The photo and the map show the
same place. Use the map to find
the lake and the park.

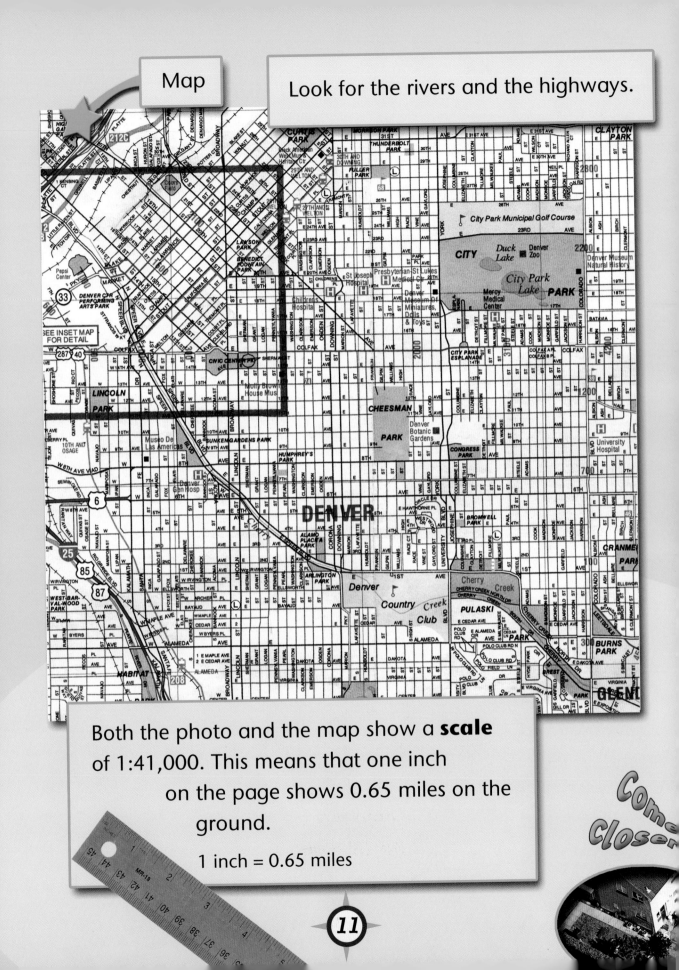

Map

Look for the rivers and the highways.

Both the photo and the map show a **scale** of 1:41,000. This means that one inch on the page shows 0.65 miles on the ground.

1 inch = 0.65 miles

Come Closer

Sam Singh
1360 Monaco Street
Denver, Colorado
United States
Planet Earth
Solar System
Universe

This is where I live.

This photo was taken from a balloon. The scale of the photo is 1:300.

There is a picnic table and bench in my yard.

Can you find my house?

Come Closer

Look Back

1. What can a map tell us that a photo can't?

2. Look for the first page where you can see cars. What is the scale of the photo?

3. Name the planets in order. Start with the one closest to the Sun.

4. What do you think the photos taken from spacecraft tell us about Earth?

5. How do you think the photo on page 10 was taken?

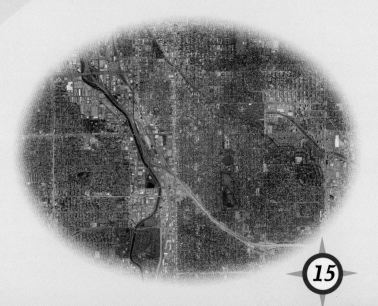

15

Index

balloon	13
city	8, 10
Earth	4, 6, 7
map	10, 11
Denver	8, 10, 11
planet	4, 5, 6, 7
satellite	9
scale	11, 13
solar system	4, 5
spacecraft	3, 7, 9
United States	6, 8, 9
universe	3

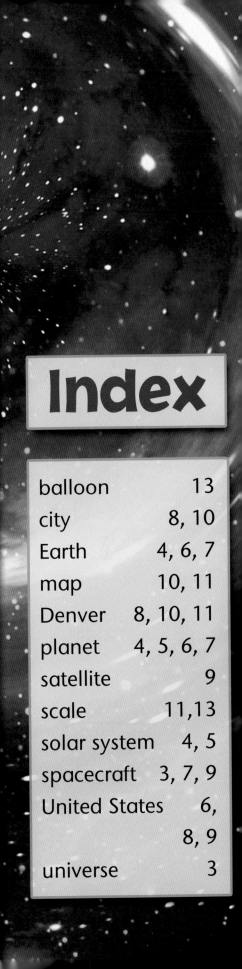

Glossary

light year — the distance that light travels in one year

planet — a large thing that travels around the Sun

satellite — a moon or spacecraft that travels around a planet

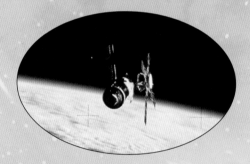

scale a set of units for measuring something

solar system — the Sun and the planets that travel around it

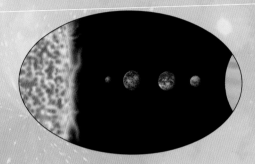

universe — all the stars, and other worlds that there are, and everything and everyone in them